To see more of our books, visit us at:
www.PuppyDogsAndIceCream.com

LEARN

FUN FACTS

SIZE

WEIGHT

LOCATION

AGES 3-10

THE FANTASTIC WORLD OF
Reptiles

Dr. Coleman M. Sheehy III of the
Florida Museum of Natural History

FUN FACTS
About Our
Scaly Friends

About the Author

Coleman holding a Glossy snake
(*Arizona elegans*).
Photo by Harvey B. Lillywhite.

My lifelong fascination with reptiles began earlier than I can remember. As a young child, I vividly remember my father asking me what I wanted to do when I grew up. I replied with the most exciting thing I could imagine, **"I want to travel to the Amazon rain-forest and find new species of reptiles!"** I exclaimed. Since then, I have spent decades traveling around the world catching and studying reptiles. I have published research papers and taught university courses on reptiles as well.

In 2014, **I found and named a new species of colorful little snake from Ecuador**, which I gave the scientific name *Siphlophis ayauma*. I currently curate one of the largest herpetological (study of reptiles) research collections in the United States.

Reptiles take such diverse forms as lizards, crocodilians, snakes, turtles, and the Tuatara. As dinosaurs, reptiles were the dominant animals on planet Earth for over 150 million years! Some modern lineages

of reptiles pre-date the dinosaurs, and **birds are now considered reptiles because they descended from dinosaurs.**

Today, with over 11,500 species found worldwide, **there are currently more species of reptiles than amphibians, birds, or even mammals.** Incredibly, several hundred species of reptiles new to science are still being discovered every year.

With this book I have attempted to showcase several species that I feel represent an interesting sample of the diversity of reptiles. It is my hope that this book will help instill in children everywhere their own lifelong fascinations with reptiles.

Dr. Coleman M. Sheehy III
Herpetology Collection Manager
Florida Museum of Natural History

To my daughters Ayla and Gabriella.
May you always have the courage to follow your dreams.

Saltwater Crocodile

Crocodylus porosus

FUN FACTS

The saltwater crocodile is the largest living reptile and has the strongest bite of any animal alive today, with a force of 3,700 pounds per square inch.

Teeth are all different sizes

They have a long, narrow snout shaped like a "v"

They have salt glands in their tongues that remove excess salt

Crocodile teeth are constantly being replaced, and they will produce about 8,000 teeth throughout their lives

Where do they live?
Coastal waters from India to Australia

How big are they?
+/- 2,000 lbs = a small car
+/- 20 feet long = 2 basketball hoops

What do they eat?
Snakes, turtles, birds, fish, and small, medium, and large mammals

American Alligator

Alligator mississippiensis

FUN FACTS

Female American alligators are caring mothers. They build nests for their eggs which they guard from predators. They even carry the young in their mouths to safely transport them from the nest to the water.

Upward-facing nostrils help it breath while staying submerged

Their backs are dark to help it blend into murky water

They have a laterally compressed tail for swimming

Alligator shouts are long, rounded, and resemble a paddle

Where do they live?
North Carolina to Florida, over to east Texas

How big are they?
+/- 500 lbs = a pig
+/- 10 feet long = a basketball hoop

What do they eat?
Fish, snails, frogs, birds, snakes, turtles, and small mammals

Komodo Dragon

Varanus komodoensis

FUN FACTS

Komodo dragons are the largest lizards alive today. Equipped with long, serrated teeth, these voracious predators can eat up to 80% of their body weight in one meal. The males engage in fierce battles for dominance.

Their long, forked tongues are used to smell their environment

Tough armored skin contains hundreds of tiny bones called osteoderms

Their large, powerful tails are often used as a weapon

Komodos have long claws on their feet

Where do they live?
Southeastern Indonesia

How big are they?
+/- 175 lbs = a washing machine
+/- 10 feet long = a basketball hoop

What do they eat?
Deer, water buffalo, wild boar, and snakes

Perentie

Varanus giganteus

FUN FACTS

The perentie is the fastest reptile, running up to speeds of 25 mph, and it is also the largest lizard in Australia. They dig large, complex burrows to both live in and hide from predators.

It can sprint on all four legs or upright on its powerful hind legs

The colors and patterns of its skin help it blend into the arid deserts where it lives

Five large claws on each foot help with digging and climbing

Its very strong tail helps keep it upright while running

Where do they live?
Australia

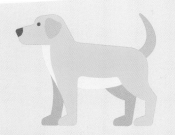

How big are they?
+/- 33 lbs = a medium dog
+/- 6 feet long = a refrigerator

What do they eat?
Insects, lizards, small mammals, birds, and sea turtle eggs

Phantastic
Leaf-Tailed Gecko

Uroplatus phantasticus

FUN FACTS

The leaf-tailed gecko is one of the best camouflaged animals on the planet. The bodies and tails of these nocturnal lizards perfectly mimic dead leaves.

Soft skin projections on its knees, elbows, and eyelids help them to camouflage

Large eyes help them see at night

Its tail is broad and shaped like a leaf

They do not have eyelids

Where do they live?
Madagascar

How big are they?
+/- 0.32 oz = a pencil
+/- 4 inches long = a crayon

What do they eat?
Insects and snails

Panther Chameleon

Furcifer pardalis

FUN FACTS

The panther chameleon changes the color of its skin depending primarily on temperature or mood. Color changes serve to communicate with other chameleons or to warn and confuse predators with vibrant patterns.

They move their eyes in separate directions

They can display an extremely colorful variety of patterns on their skin

A long, prehensile tail and fused toes help them cling to branches

To catch food they have a long, sticky, slingshot-like tongue

Where do they live?
Madagascar

How big are they?
+/- 8 oz = a baseball
+/- 17 inches long = a bowling pin

What do they eat?
Insects and spiders

Marine Iguana

Amblyrhynchus cristatus

FUN FACTS

Marine iguanas are the only species of lizard that live in marine habitats. They feed on algae that grows on the rocks underwater, and males can dive to 98 ft below the ocean surface in search of food.

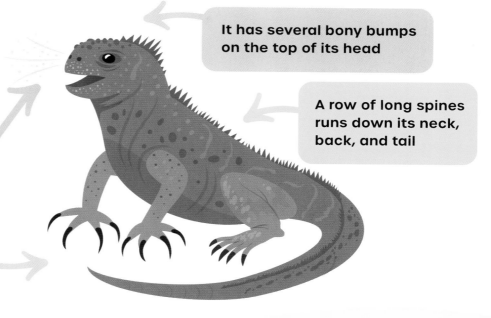

It has several bony bumps on the top of its head

A row of long spines runs down its neck, back, and tail

Excess salt in its blood is concentrated into salt glands in the nasal cavities and sneezed out, often leaving encrusted, dry, white salt on its nose and head

Long, strong claws help them cling to the lava rocks

Where do they live?
Galapagos Islands

How big are they?
+/- 12 lbs = a cat
+/- 4 feet long = a 7 year old

What do they eat?
Algae

Green Basilisk

Basiliscus plumifrons

FUN FACTS

Green basilisks have the amazing ability to run on the surface of water for 10-20 feet. They run on their hind legs using speed and specialized scales on their toes to keep them from sinking. This ability helps them to catch prey and escape predators.

They have large, triangle-shaped heads

It has several crests running along its head, back, and tail

Body is bright green with gray or light-blue markings

Its hind legs are longer than its front which help it run upright

Where do they live?
Central America

How big are they?
+/- 7 oz = a hamster
+/- 2.5 feet long = 2 bowling pins

What do they eat?
Insects, spiders, small lizards, and small mammals

Thorny Devil

Moloch horridus

FUN FACTS

The thorny devil has tiny grooves between the scales on its body that direct water to the corners of the mouth. As a result, these spiky, desert-dwelling lizards can collect and drink water by touching it with any part of the body.

Two large horns above its eyes help it defend against attacks

Thorny Devils have a "false head" on their neck to confuse predators

It is covered in hard, sharp spikes for self-defense

Its body is different shades of desert brown and tan for camouflage

Where do they live?
Australia

How big are they?
+/- 3 oz = a deck of cards
+/- 8 inches long = a piece of paper

What do they eat?
Ants

Armadillo Lizard

Ouroborus cataphractus

FUN FACTS

The armadillo lizard will protect itself from predators by biting its tail and rolling into a tight ball, making itself too difficult to swallow. These desert-dwelling lizards live among rock crevices in large family groups with individuals of all ages.

Their tail can be longer than their body

They vary from light to dark brown in color with a yellow underbelly

It has a stocky, flattened body to roll up easier

Its body is covered in heavily-armored, spiky plates

Where do they live?
South Africa

How big are they?
+/- 5 oz = a baseball

+/- 4 inches long = a crayon

What do they eat?
Insects and spiders

Cloudy Snail-Eating Snake

Sibon nebulatus

FUN FACTS

Cloudy snail-eating snakes have specialized skulls, teeth arrangements, and behaviors that allow them to quickly extract snails from their shells. Afterwards, they swallow the body of the snail and discard the empty shell.

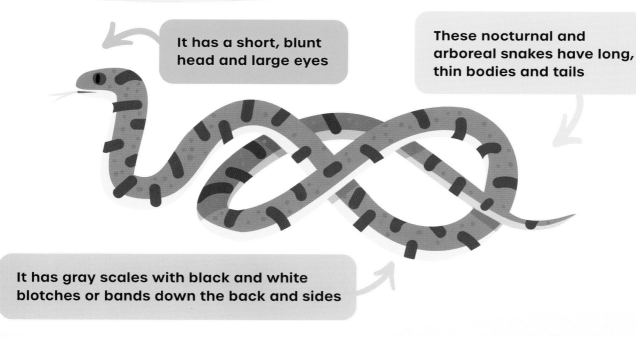

It has a short, blunt head and large eyes

These nocturnal and arboreal snakes have long, thin bodies and tails

It has gray scales with black and white blotches or bands down the back and sides

Where do they live?
Mexico, Central America, and Northern South America

How big are they?
+/- 8 oz = an orange
+/- 36 inches = an average door width

What do they eat?
Land snails and slugs

King Cobra

Ophiophagus hannah

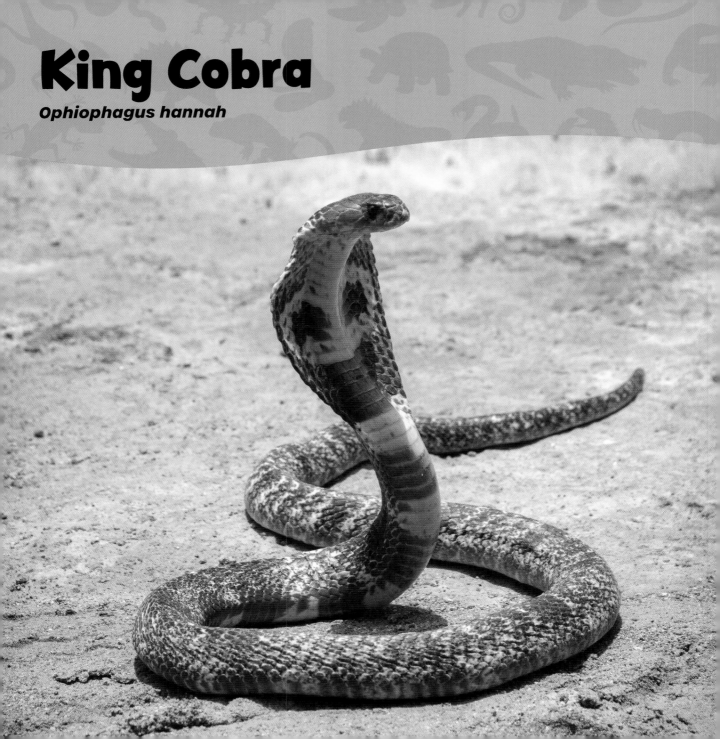

FUN FACTS

The king cobra is the longest venomous snake in the world and has been known to even stop elephants in their tracks. Females construct large nests of sticks and leaves in which they lay their eggs and guard them until they hatch.

The king cobra is most easily identified by its patterned "hood"

The hood is formed by expanding its ribs and neck, which helps it to appear more threatening to predators

The black or dark brown and yellowish-gray pattern on its hood creates false eye spots to confuse potential predators

The name Ophiophagus means "snake-eating"

Where do they live?
India, Southern Asia, and Indonesia

How big are they?
+/- 18 lbs = a bowling ball
+/- 13 feet long = a length of an elephant

What do they eat?
Snakes and lizards

Eastern
Diamondback Rattlesnake
Crotalus adamanteus

FUN FACTS

The eastern diamondback rattlesnake is the largest species of rattlesnake in the world. These predators have a pair of heat-sensitive pits on their face that allow them to locate warm-blooded prey in complete darkness.

It has a flat, triangle-shaped head

It uses its loud rattle to tell predators, other snakes, and people to stay away

Its name was given for the diamond pattern that runs along the entire length of its body

The coiled posture helps it strike fast to ambush prey

Where do they live?
Southeast US up to North Carolina

How big are they?
+/- 10 lbs = a cat
+/- 6 feet long = a refrigerator

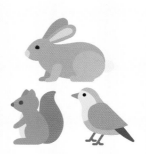

What do they eat?
Small-medium sized mammals and birds

Gaboon Viper

Bitis gabonica

FUN FACTS

The gaboon viper has the longest fangs of any venomous snake, which can grow up to 2 inches long. It is the largest viper in Africa.

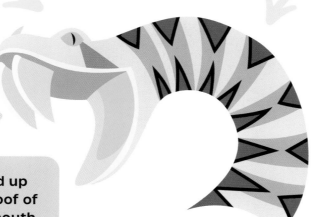

Its large, broad head mimics a dead leaf

A complex pattern of light and dark brown, pink and purple markings run along its back

The fangs fold up against the roof of the snake's mouth when not in use

Cryptic coloration helps these ambush predators blend into the forest floor

Where do they live?
Central, East, and West Africa

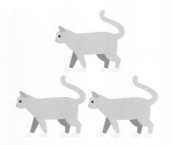

How big are they?
+/- 45 lbs = 3 cats
+/- 6 feet long = a refrigerator

What do they eat?
Small-medium sized mammals and birds

Boa Constrictor

Boa constrictor

FUN FACTS

Boa constrictors kill their prey by constriction – squeezing and suffocating – before swallowing them whole. Like all boas, boa constrictors give birth to live young as opposed to laying eggs like many other snakes.

Boa constrictors can live for over 40 years

They have tan, brown, gray, cream, black, and red markings

The patterns on its back help it blend into its environment

It is not venomous, but they have six rows of large, strong teeth

Where do they live?
Mexico, Central America, and South America

How big are they?
+/- 30 lbs = a medium size dog
+/- 10 feet long = a length of an elephant

What do they eat?
Large lizards, birds, bats, and small-medium sized mammals

Giant Tortoise

Chelonoidis nigra

FUN FACTS

Giant tortoises are the largest living species of tortoise. Their average lifespan is over 100 years, and some individuals have lived over 175 years, making them one of the longest-lived species of vertebrates on Earth.

Giant tortoises are toothless but have a sharp beak

All tortoises are turtles, but not all turtles are tortoises

Their thick, stumpy legs are able to support their massive weight

The thick scales on their skin can vary in color from gray to black

Where do they live?
Galapagos Islands

How big are they?
+/- 800 lbs = a horse
+/- 6 feet long = a refrigerator

What do they eat?
Cactus, fruits, vines, and grass

Leatherback Sea Turtle

Dermochelys coriacea

FUN FACTS

Leatherback sea turtles are the largest of all living turtles and have the longest migration of any reptile. They may travel over 10,000 miles in a single year in search of their food. They can also dive down to over 4,000 ft. They are well-adapted to surviving in cold water, and their range extends into the Arctic Circle.

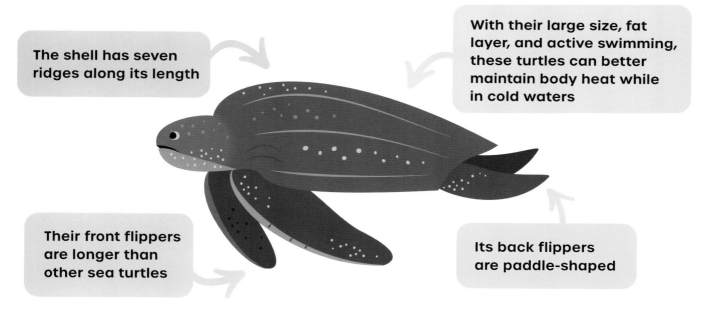

The shell has seven ridges along its length

With their large size, fat layer, and active swimming, these turtles can better maintain body heat while in cold waters

Their front flippers are longer than other sea turtles

Its back flippers are paddle-shaped

Where do they live?
The Atlantic, Pacific, and Indian Ocean

How big are they?
+/- 1,500 lbs = a cow
+/- 6 feet long = a refrigerator

What do they eat?
Jellyfish and salps

Alligator Snapping Turtle

Macrochelys temminckii

FUN FACTS

The alligator snapping turtle is the largest freshwater turtle in North America. With a bite force of 1,000 pounds per square inch, these huge turtles can bite through bone. By comparison, the bite force in humans is around 160 pounds per square inch.

Their powerful, hooked beak can bite a fish clean in half

It has a spiky shell for defense against potential predators

Its tongue looks like a worm and is wiggled underwater like a lure to bring fish closer

Its eyes are on the side of its head for a better range of vision in the murky waters

Where do they live?
North Florida to East Texas

How big are they?
+/- 160 lbs = a wolf
+/- 2.7 feet long = a cat

What do they eat?
Fish, snakes, frogs, crayfish, clams, and birds

Photograph Credits and Copyrights.

CLAIM YOUR FREE GIFT!

Visit

PDICBooks.com/Gift

Thank you for purchasing
The Fantastic World of Reptiles,
and welcome to the Puppy Dogs & Ice Cream family.

We're certain you're going to love
the little gift we've prepared for you
at the website above.